MARGARET MORGAN
and
MARY MORGAN PEDLOW

Memorial

RIVERSIDE PUBLIC LIBRARY

ANIMALS OF THE SEA AND SHORE

A TRUE BOOK

by

Ann O. Squire

Children's Press®
A Division of Scholastic Inc.

New York Toronto London Auckland Sydney
Mexico City New Delhi Hong Kong
Danbury, Connecticut

A blue-footed booby

Content Consultant
Kathy Carlstead, Ph.D.
Honolulu Zoo

Reading Consultant
Nanci R. Vargus, Ed.D.
*Primary Multiage Teacher
Decatur Township Schools,
Indianapolis, IN*

Dedication
To Emma

The photograph on the cover shows Galapagos sea lions. The photograph on the title page shows clown fish hiding in the tentacles of a sea anemone.

Library of Congress Cataloging-in-Publication Data

Squire, Ann.
    Animals of the Sea and Shore / by Ann O. Squire.
        p. cm.—(A True book)
    Includes bibliographical references (p.).
    ISBN 0-516-22190-6 (lib. bdg.)   0-516-25997-0 (pbk.)
    1. Seashore animals—Juvenile literature. [1. Seashore animals.
2. Marine animals.] I. Title. II. Series.

QL122.2 .S72 2001
591.769'9—dc21   00-057025

Contents

Crabs in the Galapagos Islands (top); a harbor seal (sitting on rock) and a herring gull (middle); a sea anemone on a coral reef in the Caribbean Sea (bottom)

Home at Sea

When you go to the beach, how many animals do you see? A crab scooting across the sand? A gull bobbing in the waves or pecking at a shell washed up on the shore? The sea and the shoreline are home to thousands of different creatures. They range from the tiniest snail to the great blue whale—and just about everything in between.

5

Mollusks

Some of the most familiar animals of the seashore are mollusks—mussels, clams, oysters, and snails. Although we rarely see these creatures alive, we often see the beautiful shells these animals leave behind when they die.

A giant clam and
a ring-top snail

Many people like to walk
along the beach and collect
mollusk shells. Although many

Many people like to collect mollusk shells.

mollusks have hard shells, all mollusks have soft bodies. In fact, the Latin word *Mollusca* means "soft."

Clams, mussels, oysters, and scallops are called bivalves

because they have two hard shells joined by a kind of hinge. When they feel threatened, these creatures clamp their shells tightly shut.

Mussels (left), clams (bottom left), and oysters (bottom right) are bivalves.

Periwinkle snails clinging to stones

Snails are mollusks too, but they have only one shell, often coiled into a spiral shape. The periwinkle is a sea snail that clings to rocks with one strong sucker-like foot.

A squid in front of coral

Squid and octopus are also mollusks, though they look very different from mollusks with shells. The octopus's body is so soft and flexible that it can squeeze into the tiniest underwater crevices to look for food or shelter.

Both squid and octopus swim backward by shooting out jets of water, but the octopus can also use its eight long tentacles to pull itself forward. The octopus's tentacles are covered with round disks that work like suction cups. An octopus can use its powerful tentacles to

An octopus (below) and a close-up view of the disks on an octopus's tentacles (left)

climb out of a glass aquarium
or pry open an oyster shell
for its meat.

Crustaceans

Lobsters, crabs, and shrimp are residents of the seashore as well, though you may see them more often on your dinner plate than at the beach. These animals belong to a group called *Crustacea*, which means "with a crust or shell."

Shrimp are crustaceans.

In many ways, crustaceans are like insects. Both have a tough outer skeleton, antennae, and many legs. But while most insects live on dry land, crustaceans are usually found in salt water.

Lobsters eat clams, sea stars, and even algae and seagrass. Next time you see a lobster in the grocery store, notice that its two large claws have differ-ent shapes. The long, slender claw is lined with sharp "teeth." This claw is meant for grabbing and tearing prey. The shorter claw is designed for holding and crushing food.

The hermit crab has no shell of its own, so it lives in the empty shell of another creature. When the hermit crab grows

A hermit crab

too big for its home, it simply looks around for a roomier shell and moves right in. The shell it leaves behind may become the cozy home of a smaller hermit crab.

One crustacean that looks nothing like the others is the barnacle. You may have seen the little volcano-shaped shells of barnacles clinging to wooden docks at low tide. When the tide rises again, it covers the barnacles with

Barnacles clinging to a pier (above) and a barnacle feeding (right)

water. Then these little animals stretch out their feathery "legs" to catch any tiny bits of food that may float by.

Birds of the Beach

Whenever you visit the seashore, you're sure to see lots of large, gray-and-white birds. They may be circling in the sky or searching for food along the beach. Like most people, you probably call these birds "seagulls," but their real name is herring gull. Herring gulls eat almost anything they

Creatures of the Shallows and the Deep

Some of the strangest sea animals live beneath the water's surface. The flounder, for example, is a flat fish that has both its eyes on the same side of its head! Why?

A flounder is born with its eyes on either side of its head,

A flounder has both eyes on the same side of its head.

like other fish. But a flounder swims along the seafloor with one side of its body facing down into the sand. As it gets used to swimming along the bottom, one eye changes sides, so that the flounder has both eyes looking up.

Another weird-looking creature is the hammerhead shark. Its eyes and nostrils are on opposite ends of its wide, hammer-shaped head. Some scientists think that its widely spaced nostrils help the shark home in on the scent of its prey. Hammerheads can grow up to 20 feet (6 meters) long and have been known to

A hammerhead shark near Costa Rica

attack humans. They also eat fish, stingrays, and other sharks.

A Long, Long Tail

The thresher shark has a tail that grows as long as the rest of its body. That means that an 18-ft. (5.5-m) shark has a tail that is 9 ft. (2.7 m) long! Thresher sharks use their huge, curving tails to herd schools of fish into groups so that they are easier to catch. A thresher shark may also stun a fish by hitting it with its tail.

Marine Mammals

Many creatures that live in the sea are mammals. Unlike fish, mammals are warm-blooded, so their bodies need to be designed to keep them warm in the cold ocean water.

Sea otters have very thick fur that keeps them warm. California sea otters spend

An elephant seal

almost all their time in the water, swimming and resting. They even sleep in the water, on their backs!

Sea otters grooming
themselves

Sea otters also spend a lot
of time grooming their fur. Oil
spills are especially dangerous
for sea otters, because the oil
soaks their fur and they can no
longer keep warm.

Walruses, seals, and sea lions depend on a thick layer of blubber to keep them warm. A walrus's blubber can be up to 6 inches (15 centimeters) thick.

Walruses have a thick layer of blubber to keep them warm.

The blue whale is the largest
animal in the world. It grows up
to 85 ft. (26 m) long. A blue
whale's heart alone can weigh
2,000 pounds (907 kilograms)—
as much as a small car.

Whales, otters, seals, and
other marine mammals have

Sea lions can stay underwater for many minutes (above), but eventually, they must come up for air (left).

something else in common: they all breathe air. So no matter how deep they dive or how long they stay down, they must rise to the surface to take a breath.

Plant or Animal?

In this book, we have met many unusual animals of the sea and the shore, but all of them have looked like animals. Some animals of the tropical seas, however, look like flowers, fans, or even rocks.

Have you ever seen those lumpy brown sponges that

Although they look like plants, coral and sea fans (left) and sponges (above) are animals.

people sometimes use in the bath? Did you know that this kind of sponge is actually an animal? Sponges eat by sucking water into their many holes and filtering out tiny creatures called plankton.

Sea stars (left), sea urchins (top right), and sand dollars (bottom right)

Sea stars, sand dollars, and sea urchins are animals called echinoderms. An echinoderm's body can be divided into five parts surrounding a central point—somewhat like a star.

Echinoderms have hard, external skeletons, often covered with warty skin or spines. They are often found in tide pools, where they cling to rocks and move around on tiny tube feet. You may have heard that if a sea star's arm is accidentally cut off, the animal can grow a new one. But did you know that just one arm can grow into a whole new sea star?

Many tropical seas have islands and reefs made of coral.

A coral reef in the South Pacific (left) and a close-up view of coral polyps (right)

Coral reefs may look like sharp rocks, but they are actually made up of millions of tiny sea creatures called coral polyps. Each polyp lives inside a small rocky skeleton. When the polyps die, their skeletons are left behind and new coral polyps grow on top of them. Coral reefs are formed in this way over thousands of years.

Looking more like a brightly colored flower than an animal, the sea anemone is a common

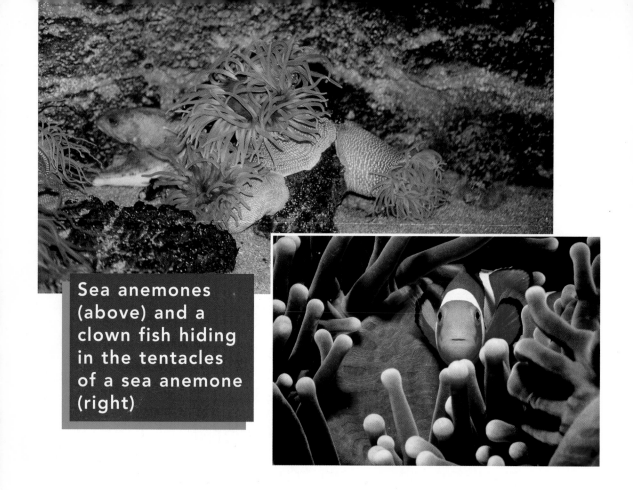

Sea anemones
(above) and a
clown fish hiding
in the tentacles
of a sea anemone
(right)

sight on the coral reef. An anemone does not move around in search of food. Instead, it stays in one place and waits for food to come swimming by.

The anemone has a secret weapon—its tentacles. They look like beautiful flower petals as they sway in the current. But these tentacles are deadly, delivering a powerful sting to almost any fish that swims too close.

The clown fish is one of the few creatures not affected by an anemone's stings, because it has a special slime covering its body. Clown fish often live among the anemone's tentacles, where they are safe from larger fish that might try to eat them.

To Find Out More

Here are some additional resources to help you learn more about animals of the sea and shore:

 **Books**

Blum, Mark. **Coral Reef** (Eye to Eye Books). Somerville House, 1998.

Johnson, Jinny. **Children's Guide to Sea Creatures.** Simon & Schuster, 1998.

Maynard, Christopher. **Informania: Sharks.** Candlewick Press, 1997.

Telford, Carole, and Theodorou, Rod. **Inside a Coral Reef.** Heinemann Interactive Library, 1998.

Totally Amazing Sea Creatures. Golden Books, 1998.

Organizations and Online Sites

Aquatic Network
http://www.aquanet.com/

A great site with general information about oceans and close-ups on such interesting topics as sharks, ocean exploration, and conservation.

The Evergreen Project— Marine Ecosystems
http://www.mobot.org/ MBGnet/salt/

Visit this web-based education site to learn about life in the ocean.

Monterey Bay Aquarium
886 Cannery Row
Monterey, CA 93940
http://www.mbayaq.org

This is a great place to learn all about marine animals. At the aquarium's website, you can take the Habitat Path to explore coastal environments, go "into" exhibits, or dive deep into the Monterey Canyon on a virtual expedition.

National Geographic
http://www. nationalgeographic.com

Lots of interesting information on animals and nature for kids and adults.

Discovery Channel
http://www.Animal. Discovery.com

Information on all kinds of animals, and links to nature shows on the Discovery Channel.

Important Words

blubber thick layer of fat underneath the skin of whales and other sea mammals

crevices narrow openings

current water or air moving in one direction

expandable something that is able to open up or get bigger

mammal animal that is warm-blooded, breathes air, has hair or fur, and has babies fed with milk from the mother

oil spill accident in which a ship carrying oil or an offshore oil well spills large amounts of oil into the sea

plankton tiny plants and animals that live in the water and are food for many fish

prey animal hunted by another animal for food

warm-blooded able to maintain a high and constant body temperature whether the surroundings are warm or cold

Index

Meet the Author

Ann O. Squire has a Ph.D. in animal behavior. Before becoming a writer, she studied African electric fish, rats, and other animals. Dr. Squire has written several books on animals and their behavior, including *Anteaters, Sloths, and Armadillos* and *Spiders of North America*. She lives with her children, Emma and Evan, in Bedford, New York.